KU-178-326

2017 SQA Past Papers with Answers

National 5
FRENCH

FREE
audio files to accompany this
title can be accessed at
**www.hoddereducation.co.uk/
sqaaudiofiles**
You will find the files listed by
language and level.

2015, 2016 & 2017 Exams

HODDER
GIBSON
AN HACHETTE UK COMPANY

This book contains the official SQA 2015, 2016 and 2017 Exams for National 5 French, with associated SQA-approved answers modified from the official marking instructions that accompany the paper.

In addition the book contains study skills advice. This advice has specially commissioned by Hodder Gibson, and has been written by experienced senior teachers and examiners in line with the new National 5 syllabus and assessment outlines. This is not SQA material but has been devised to provide further guidance for National 5 examinations.

Hodder Gibson is grateful to the copyright holders, as credited on the final page of the Answer section, for permission to use their material. Every effort has been made to trace the copyright holders and to obtain their permission for the use of copyright material. Hodder Gibson will be happy to receive information allowing us to rectify any error or omission in future editions.

Hachette UK's policy is to use papers that are natural, renewable and recyclable products and made from wood grown in sustainable forests. The logging and manufacturing processes are expected to conform to the environmental regulations of the country of origin.

Orders: please contact Bookpoint Ltd, 130 Park Drive, Milton Park, Abingdon, Oxon OX14 4SE. Telephone: (44) 01235 827720. Fax: (44) 01235 400454. Lines are open 9.00–5.00, Monday to Saturday, with a 24-hour message answering service. Visit our website at www.hoddereducation.co.uk. Hodder Gibson can be contacted direct on: Tel: 0141 333 4650; Fax: 0141 404 8188; email: hoddergibson@hodder.co.uk

This collection first published in 2017 by
Hodder Gibson, an imprint of Hodder Education,
An Hachette UK Company
211 St Vincent Street
Glasgow G2 5QY

National 5 2015, 2016 and 2017 Exam Papers and Answers © Scottish Qualifications Authority. Study Skills section © Hodder Gibson. All rights reserved. Apart from any use permitted under UK copyright law, no part of this publication may be reproduced or transmitted in any form or by any means, electronic or mechanical, including photocopying and recording, or held within any information storage and retrieval system, without permission in writing from the publisher or under licence from the Copyright Licensing Agency Limited. Further details of such licences (for reprographic reproduction) may be obtained from the Copyright Licensing Agency Limited, www.cla.co.uk.

Typeset by Aptara, Inc.

Printed in the UK

A catalogue record for this title is available from the British Library

ISBN: 978-1-5104-2182-0

2 1

2018 2017

Introduction

National 5 French

The course specifications for National 5 French have changed, and Units and Unit Assessments have been removed. The only change to the exam papers, however, is the removal of 'overall purpose' questions for Reading and Listening. The Past Papers have been altered to reflect this, so these remain current and incredibly useful tools for your revision. The exams contained in this book of Past Papers provide excellent representative exam practice. Using them as part of your revision will help you to learn the vital skills and techniques needed for the exam, and will help you to identify any knowledge gaps you may have, prior to the exam season in May–June.

The course

The National 5 French course aims to enable you to develop the ability to read, listen, talk and write in French, that is to understand and use French, and to apply your knowledge and understanding of the language. The course offers the opportunity to develop detailed language skills in the real-life contexts of society, learning, employability and culture.

How the course is graded

The Course assessment will take the form of a performance, a writing assignment and a written exam.

The performance will be a presentation and discussion with your teacher, which will be recorded and marked by your teacher. It is worth 25% of your final mark.

The topic for the writing assignment will be agreed between you and your teacher. It will be carried out in class, under supervised conditions. It is worth 12.5% of your final mark.

This book will help you practise for the written exam you will sit in May.

The exams

Reading and Writing

- exam time: 1 hour 30 minutes
- total marks: 50
- weighting in final grade: 37.5%

What you have to do

- Read three passages of just under 200 words each, and answer questions about them in English.
- write 120–200 words in French in the form of an email, applying for a job or work placement: there will be six bullet points for you to address.

Listening

- exam time: 25 minutes
- total marks: 20
- weighting in final grade: 25%

What you have to do

- part 1: listen to a monologue in French, and answer questions in English
- part 2: listen to a dialogue In French, and answer questions about it in English.

How to improve your mark!

Every year, examiners notice the same kind of mistakes being made, and also they regularly come across some excellent work. They give advice in the three key areas of reading, listening and writing to help students do better. Here are some key points from their advice.

Reading

Make sure that your answers include detail in Reading. Remember, an answer of only one word will not normally be enough to gain a mark. However, you do not have to answer in sentences; bullet points are fine. Pick out detail from longer chunks of language, rather than focusing on individual words. Read the whole message, then pick out the key points, using the questions as a guide as to where to look. Detailed answers are generally required, so pay particular attention to words like *assez*, *très*, *trop*, *vraiment* and to negatives. Make sure you get the details of numbers, day, times, etc. right.

Take care when using dictionaries where a word has more than one meaning. Learn to choose the correct meaning from a list of meanings in a dictionary.

Beware of *faux amis*: *journée* means day, not journey, *travailler* means work, not travel, for instance!

In responding to the questions in the Reading papers, you should be guided by the number of points awarded for each question. You should give as much detail in your answer as you have understood but should not put down everything which is in the original text, as you are wasting time. The question itself usually indicates the amount of information required by stating in bold, e.g. "State **two** things" or "Give **any two**". If the question says "state any two things", it means that there are more than two possibilities. Just choose the two you are happiest with and stick to them. Only give alternatives if you are absolutely unsure of what is correct.

If you have time at the end, you should re-read your answers to make sure that they make sense and that your English expression is as good as it can be.

Listening

This is the paper that improves most with practice. So use the Listening papers in this book several times, to get used to the format of the exam.

Not giving enough detail is still a major reason for candidates losing marks. Many answers are correct as far as they go but were not sufficiently detailed to score marks. The same rules as for Reading apply.

You hear each of the Listening texts three times, so make use of the third listening to check the accuracy and specific details of your answers.

Be sure you are able to give accurate answers through confident knowledge of numbers, common adjectives, weather expressions, prepositions and question words, so that some of the "easier" points of information are not lost through lack of sufficiently accurate details.

In responding to the questions in the Listening papers, you should be guided by the number of points awarded for each question, and by the wording of the question. You should give as much detail in your answer as you have understood but should not write down everything you hear. The question itself usually indicates the amount of information required by stating in bold, e.g. "State **two** of them".

Make sure you put a line through any notes you have made.

Writing

This, along with Talking, is where students do best. It is a chance for you to know what your answers to the first four bullet points are in advance. Make sure you have some good material prepared and learned, ready to use in the exam.

Also, where learners write pieces that are too lengthy, this certainly does not help their performance. So stick to the 20–30 words per bullet point.

The examiners say many of the pieces are vibrant and refreshing in terms of style and content. At the upper level, the majority of candidates write well, and the range of language used is impressive. So look at the success criteria in the Answer section and try to model your writing on it. This applies particularly to the last two bullet points. Practise writing answers to the final two bullet points, which are different in every exam, adapting material you already know rather than using a dictionary to translate ideas from English.

You should ensure that you are careful when you read the information regarding the job you are applying for, and make sure your answer is tailored to fit that. Depending on the job, you may have to alter your strengths or the experience you are claiming. You should prepare in French a description of some "soft" skills that

are transferable, for instance, working with the public, able to communicate, good at working as part of a team or with others.

You should avoid writing long lists of things such as school subjects (and then repeating the list with a past or future verb tense) as part of your answers.

Use the dictionary to check the accuracy of what you have written (spelling, accents, genders, etc.) but not to create new sentences, particularly when dealing with the last two bullet points. You should have everything you need prepared when you come into the exam.

Be aware of the extended criteria to be used in assessing performances in Writing, so that you know what is required in terms of content, accuracy and range and variety of language to achieve the good and very good categories. Ensure that your handwriting is legible (particularly when writing in French) and distinguish clearly between rough notes and what you wish to be considered as final answers. Make sure you score out your notes!

You should bear the following points in mind:

- there are six bullet points to answer: the first four are always the same, the last two vary from year to year
- each of the first four bullet points should have between 25 and 30 words to address it properly
- answering the first four bullet points correctly will get you 12/20. Each of the last two, if answered correctly, will get an additional 4 marks
- you should aim to write about 20 words for each of these last two points, but do not try to write too much, as this might mean you are more likely to get things wrong
- you will be assessed on how well you have answered the points, and on the accuracy of your language
- you should also try to have a variety of tenses in your preparation for the first four bullet points, including past, future and conditional if you can
- for a mark of good or very good, you should have some complex language, such as longer, varied sentences and conjunctions, so have some sub-clauses ready, starting with words like "et", "ou", "mais", "parce que", "quand", etc.

Good luck!

Remember that the rewards for passing National 5 French are well worth it! Your pass will help you get the future you want for yourself. In the exam, be confident in your own ability. If you're not sure how to answer a question, trust your instincts and just give it a go anyway – keep calm and don't panic! GOOD LUCK!

Study Skills – what you need to know to pass exams!

Pause for thought

Many students might skip quickly through a page like this. After all, we all know how to revise. Do you really though?

Think about this:

"IF YOU ALWAYS DO WHAT YOU ALWAYS DO, YOU WILL ALWAYS GET WHAT YOU HAVE ALWAYS GOT."

Do you like the grades you get? Do you want to do better? If you get full marks in your assessment, then that's great! Change nothing! This section is just to help you get that little bit better than you already are.

There are two main parts to the advice on offer here. The first part highlights fairly obvious things but which are also very important. The second part makes suggestions about revision that you might not have thought about but which WILL help you.

Part 1

DOH! It's so obvious but …

Start revising in good time

Don't leave it until the last minute – this will make you panic.

Make a revision timetable that sets out work time AND play time.

Sleep and eat!

Obvious really, and very helpful. Avoid arguments or stressful things too – even games that wind you up. You need to be fit, awake and focused!

Know your place!

Make sure you know exactly **WHEN and WHERE** your exams are.

Know your enemy!

Make sure you know what to expect in the exam.

How is the paper structured?

How much time is there for each question?

What types of question are involved?

Which topics seem to come up time and time again?

Which topics are your strongest and which are your weakest?

Are all topics compulsory or are there choices?

Learn by DOING!

There is no substitute for past papers and practice papers – they are simply essential! Tackling this collection of papers and answers is exactly the right thing to be doing as your exams approach.

Part 2

People learn in different ways. Some like low light, some bright. Some like early morning, some like evening / night. Some prefer warm, some prefer cold. But everyone uses their BRAIN and the brain works when it is active. Passive learning – sitting gazing at notes – is the most INEFFICIENT way to learn anything. Below you will find tips and ideas for making your revision more effective and maybe even more enjoyable. What follows gets your brain active, and active learning works!

Activity 1 – Stop and review

Step 1

When you have done no more than 5 minutes of revision reading STOP!

Step 2

Write a heading in your own words which sums up the topic you have been revising.

Step 3

Write a summary of what you have revised in no more than two sentences. Don't fool yourself by saying, "I know it, but I cannot put it into words". That just means you don't know it well enough. If you cannot write your summary, revise that section again, knowing that you must write a summary at the end of it. Many of you will have notebooks full of blue/black ink writing. Many of the pages will not be especially attractive or memorable so try to liven them up a bit with colour as you are reviewing and rewriting. **This is a great memory aid, and memory is the most important thing.**

Activity 2 – Use technology!

Why should everything be written down? Have you thought about "mental" maps, diagrams, cartoons and colour to help you learn? And rather than write down notes, why not record your revision material?

What about having a text message revision session with friends? Keep in touch with them to find out how and what they are revising and share ideas and questions.

Why not make a video diary where you tell the camera what you are doing, what you think you have learned and what you still have to do? No one has to see or hear it, but the process of having to organise your thoughts in a formal way to explain something is a very important learning practice.

Be sure to make use of electronic files. You could begin to summarise your class notes. Your typing might be slow, but it will get faster and the typed notes will be easier to read than the scribbles in your class notes. Try to add different fonts and colours to make your work stand out. You can easily Google relevant pictures, cartoons and diagrams which you can copy and paste to make your work more attractive and **MEMORABLE**.

Activity 3 – This is it. Do this and you will know lots!

Step 1

In this task you must be very honest with yourself! Find the SQA syllabus for your subject (www.sqa.org.uk). Look at how it is broken down into main topics called MANDATORY knowledge. That means stuff you MUST know.

Step 2

BEFORE you do ANY revision on this topic, write a list of everything that you already know about the subject. It might be quite a long list but you only need to write it once. It shows you all the information that is already in your long-term memory so you know what parts you do not need to revise!

Step 3

Pick a chapter or section from your book or revision notes. Choose a fairly large section or a whole chapter to get the most out of this activity.

With a buddy, use Skype, Facetime, Twitter or any other communication you have, to play the game "If this is the answer, what is the question?". For example, if you are revising Geography and the answer you provide is "meander", your buddy would have to make up a question like "What is the word that describes a feature of a river where it flows slowly and bends often from side to side?".

Make up 10 "answers" based on the content of the chapter or section you are using. Give this to your buddy to solve while you solve theirs.

Step 4

Construct a wordsearch of at least 10 × 10 squares. You can make it as big as you like but keep it realistic. Work together with a group of friends. Many apps allow you to make wordsearch puzzles online. The words and phrases can go in any direction and phrases can be split. Your puzzle must only contain facts linked to the topic you are revising. Your task is to find 10 bits of information to hide in your puzzle, but you must not repeat information that you used in Step 3. DO NOT show where the words are. Fill up empty squares with random letters. Remember to keep a note of where your answers are hidden but do not show your friends. When you have a complete puzzle, exchange it with a friend to solve each other's puzzle.

Step 5

Now make up 10 questions (not "answers" this time) based on the same chapter used in the previous two tasks. Again, you must find NEW information that you have not yet used. Now it's getting hard to find that new information! Again, give your questions to a friend to answer.

Step 6

As you have been doing the puzzles, your brain has been actively searching for new information. Now write a NEW LIST that contains only the new information you have discovered when doing the puzzles. Your new list is the one to look at repeatedly for short bursts over the next few days. Try to remember more and more of it without looking at it. After a few days, you should be able to add words from your second list to your first list as you increase the information in your long-term memory.

FINALLY! Be inspired...

Make a list of different revision ideas and beside each one write **THINGS I HAVE** tried, **THINGS I WILL** try and **THINGS I MIGHT** try. Don't be scared of trying something new.

And remember – "FAIL TO PREPARE AND PREPARE TO FAIL!"

NATIONAL 5

2015

N5

National
Qualifications
2015

Mark

X730/75/01

**French
Reading**

FRIDAY, 22 MAY
9:00 AM – 10:30 AM

Fill in these boxes and read what is printed below.

Full name of centre

Town

Forename(s)

Surname

Number of seat

Date of birth

Day	Month	Year

Scottish candidate number

Total marks — 30

Attempt ALL questions.

Write your answers clearly, in **English**, in the spaces provided in this booklet.

You may use a French dictionary.

Additional space for answers is provided at the end of this booklet. If you use this space you must clearly identify the question number you are attempting.

Use **blue** or **black** ink.

There is a separate question and answer booklet for Writing. You must complete your answer for Writing in the question and answer booklet for Writing.

Before leaving the examination room you must give both booklets to the Invigilator; if you do not, you may lose all the marks for this paper.

MARKS | DO NOT WRITE IN THIS MARGIN

Total marks — 30

Attempt ALL questions

Text 1

Your friend shows you an article in a French newspaper.

Les petits boulots : mode d'emploi

Lola est une collégienne de quinze ans. Elle voudrait travailler pour payer ses vêtements et pour mettre de l'argent de côté pour un voyage. Cependant ce n'est pas très facile pour les jeunes de trouver du travail.

«Personne ne veut me donner du travail! J'ai demandé à une copine de ma mère qui tient un magasin et j'ai même appelé le patron d'une grande entreprise! On m'a dit que j'étais trop jeune et ils m'ont conseillé d'attendre deux ou trois ans. Ce n'est pas juste!!»

Lola n'est pas la seule. La loi en France est très stricte. Les jeunes de moins de seize ans ne peuvent travailler que pendant les vacances scolaires et seulement si ces vacances durent quinze jours ou plus. On ne peut pas travailler plus de cinq heures par jour.

Alors, que doit-on faire pour gagner un peu d'argent?

Et bien, il faut profiter de la famille et des voisins! Aider des personnes âgées à faire des tâches ménagères, donner des cours particuliers à des élèves plus jeunes ou encore tondre le gazon. Mais attention – pour pratiquer tous ces petits boulots, il vous faudra une autorisation parentale. Comme la vie est dure!

Questions

(a) Lola would like to find a job. Why? Complete the sentence.   2

She would like to find a job to pay for her _clothes_____

and put some money away for _a trip_____.

(b) Lola talks about her job search. What did she do to find a job? State **two** things.   2

She spoke to her mother's friend and phoned the boss of a large company.

MARKS | DO NOT WRITE IN THIS MARGIN

Text 1 Questions (continued)

(c) Employers told her she was too young. What advice did they give her?   **1**

They told her to wait two or three years.

(d) The law in France is very strict for workers under the age of sixteen. What are the rules? State any **two** things.   **2**

Only if the school holidays are 15 days or more and children cannot work for more than 5 hours a day.

(e) The article suggests you can do some work for your family or neighbours. What could you do? State **three** things.   **3**

Do chores for the elderly, tutor younger students and mow the grass

[Turn over

MARKS | DO NOT WRITE IN THIS MARGIN

Text 2

You read an article which talks about the use of the Internet to support learning.

Internet et les études

L'usage d'Internet est devenu de plus en plus répandu à travers la France et on dit que c'est un outil de travail indispensable de nos jours. Les avantages sont nombreux – les étudiants peuvent faire des recherches et communiquer avec les gens partout dans le monde, tout en apprenant l'informatique.

La plupart des parents parlent aussi des bénéfices de l'Internet pour aider leurs enfants avec leurs devoirs. Par exemple, l'enfant peut essayer de trouver de l'aide par lui-même ou ses parents peuvent se renseigner pour informer l'enfant.

Néanmoins, il y a aussi des aspects négatifs: en passant des heures devant un écran on perd le contact avec la réalité et on lit moins de livres. Certaines personnes sortent de moins en moins car ils préfèrent rester chez eux à discuter avec leurs amis virtuels. Et attention! Il ne faut pas toujours croire à tout ce qu'on lit sur Internet.

Quant aux professeurs . . . oui, ils voient les avantages apportés par l'internet mais plusieurs problèmes se présentent. Par exemple, il n'y a pas assez d'ordinateurs dans les salles de classe, le système d'informatique est souvent en panne et il est parfois difficile d'accéder aux sites intéressants à l'école.

Questions

(a) The Internet has become more and more widespread in France. Which statement supports this? Tick (✓) the correct box.   1

People work more at home on the Internet.	
The Internet is an essential tool at work.	✓
You can book your travel in advance using the Internet.	

(b) What are the advantages of the Internet for students? State any **two** things.   2

They can communicate with people all over the world. They can use it for research.

MARKS | DO NOT WRITE IN THIS MARGIN

Text 2 Questions (continued)

(c) Young people often use the Internet to help with their homework. What benefits do parents see in this? State any **one** thing.

They can try to find help themselves.

1

(d) There are some negative aspects of using the Internet.

    (i) What could happen if you spend hours on the computer? State any **one** thing.

lose contact with reality,

1

    (ii) People are going out less. Why?

They prefer to stay at home to talk with their virtual friends.

1

    (iii) What do you need to be careful of when you are on the Internet?

You shouldn't believe everything you read on the internet.

1

(e) Teachers highlight a number of problems. What are they? State any **two** things.

· There aren't enough computers in classrooms

· It's ~~someth~~ sometimes difficult to access interesting sites in school

2

(f) What is the author's overall opinion about the Internet to support learning? Tick (✓) the correct box.

1

The Internet should be forbidden in schools.	
All learning should be done using the Internet.	
The Internet can support learning when and where appropriate.	✓

[Turn over

Text 3

You read an article about food waste.

C'est quoi, le gaspillage alimentaire*?

Le gaspillage alimentaire commence dès la production. Les supermarchés veulent vendre seulement de beaux produits, par exemple, des tomates bien rondes ou des pommes parfaites! Ceci oblige les producteurs de fruits et légumes à faire une sélection stricte et par conséquent, les fruits et légumes qui ont le moindre défaut finissent à la poubelle.

Le gaspillage vient aussi de nos habitudes de consommation. Bien souvent, nous achetons plus que ce que nous consommons réellement, et on jette environ 20% des aliments achetés.

Quelles sont les conséquences de ce gaspillage?

D'abord, l'argent utilisé pour produire ces aliments est gâché. Ensuite, il faut traiter tous ces déchets. Finalement, ce recyclage est une activité qui demande beaucoup d'énergie.

Que peut-on faire pour réduire le gaspillage?

Il existe des solutions très simples pour moins gaspiller à la maison: on devrait faire une liste des courses et n'acheter que la quantité de produits nécessaires. N'oubliez pas: on peut toujours congeler ce qui reste au frigo.

*Le gaspillage alimentaire — food waste

Questions

(a) Complete the following sentence. 1

Supermarkets only want to sell beautiful produce such as really round

tomatoes and _perfect apples!_ .

(b) Supermarket policy affects fruit and vegetable producers.

(i) What do the producers have to do? 1

strictly select fruit and vegetables

(ii) What happens because of this? 1

the fruit and vegetables that have the slightest defect end up in the bin

MARKS | DO NOT WRITE IN THIS MARGIN

Text 3 Questions (continued)

(c) In what ways do the habits of consumers contribute to the amount of food waste? State **two** things.   **2**

People buy more than they need and throw 20% of food away.

(d) Wasting food has consequences. State any **two** examples of this.   **2**

Money used for producing fruit and veg is wasted. Recycling demands a lot of energy.

(e) What can each household do to help? State **three** things.   **3**

Make a shopping list, only buy whats necessary and freeze leftovers for later.

[END OF QUESTION PAPER]

MARKS | DO NOT WRITE IN THIS MARGIN

ADDITIONAL SPACE FOR ANSWERS

ADDITIONAL SPACE FOR ANSWERS

MARKS | DO NOT WRITE IN THIS MARGIN

Page nine

[BLANK PAGE]

DO NOT WRITE ON THIS PAGE

FOR OFFICIAL USE

N5

National
Qualifications
2015

Mark

X730/75/02

French
Writing

FRIDAY, 22 MAY
9:00 AM – 10:30 AM

Fill in these boxes and read what is printed below.

Full name of centre

Town

Forename(s)

Surname

Number of seat

Date of birth

Day   Month   Year

Scottish candidate number

Total marks — 20

Write your answer clearly, in **French**, in the space provided in this booklet.

You may use a French dictionary.

Additional space for answers is provided at the end of this booklet.

Use **blue** or **black** ink.

There is a separate question and answer booklet for Reading. You must complete your answers for Reading in the question and answer booklet for Reading.

Before leaving the examination room you must give both booklets to the Invigilator; if you do not, you may lose all the marks for this paper.

Total marks — 20

You are preparing an application for the job advertised below and you write an e-mail in **French** to the company.

Colonie de Vacances
Pour les enfants 5 – 14 ans

Le travail en plein air vous attire?

Vous aimez travailler en équipe?

Vous êtes dynamique?

Vous aimez les enfants?

Le Jardin des Enfants en Normandie

Cherche

animateur/animatrice

Pour les mois de juin à septembre

On vous attend!

To help you to write your e-mail, you have been given the following checklist.
You must include **all** of these points

- Personal details (name, age, where you live)
- School/college/education experience until now
- Skills/interests you have which make you right for the job
- Related work experience
- The reasons why you would like to work with children
- An enquiry about what there is to do in the area on your days off

Use all of the above to help you write the e-mail in **French**. The e-mail should be approximately 120–150 words. You may use a French dictionary.

ANSWER SPACE

ANSWER SPACE (continued)

MARKS | DO NOT WRITE IN THIS MARGIN

ANSWER SPACE (continued)

ANSWER SPACE (continued)

[END OF QUESTION PAPER]

MARKS | DO NOT WRITE IN THIS MARGIN

ADDITIONAL SPACE FOR ANSWERS

MARKS | DO NOT WRITE IN THIS MARGIN

ADDITIONAL SPACE FOR ANSWERS

N5

National
Qualifications
2015

Mark

X730/75/03

**French
Listening**

FRIDAY, 22 MAY

10:50 AM – 11:15 AM (approx)

Fill in these boxes and read what is printed below.

Full name of centre

Town

Forename(s)

Surname

Number of seat

Date of birth

Day	Month	Year

Scottish candidate number

Total marks — 20

Attempt ALL questions.

You will hear two items in French. **Before you hear each item, you will have one minute to study the questions.** You will hear each item three times, with an interval of one minute between playings. You will then have time to answer the questions before hearing the next item.

You may NOT use a French dictionary.

Write your answers clearly, in **English**, in the spaces provided in this booklet. Additional space for answers is provided at the end of this booklet. If you use this space you must clearly identify the question number you are attempting.

Use **blue** or **black** ink.

You are not allowed to leave the examination room until the end of the test.

Before leaving the examination room you must give this booklet to the Invigilator; if you do not, you may lose all the marks for this paper.

MARKS | DO NOT WRITE IN THIS MARGIN

Total marks — 20

Attempt ALL questions

Item 1

Whilst in France you listen to a young actor who is speaking on a local radio station.

(a) When did the film festival start?

1

(b) What will a 30 Euro ticket allow you to do? State any **one** thing.

1

(c) You can see the films in their original language. What are the advantages of this? State **two** things.

2

(d) After some films you can take part in a debate. What will you have the chance to do there? State any **two** things.

2

(e) The actor talks about her film. What is it about? State any **one** thing.

1

(f) What is the purpose of the film festival? Tick (✓) the correct box.

1

To make money	
To promote international films	
To encourage young people to become actors	

Item 2

MARKS

Christophe talks to Julie about French cinema and television.

(a) Why is Julie really happy? State any **one** thing.

1

_____

(b) What does Julie love about going to the cinema? Tick (✓) the **two** correct boxes.

2

Eating popcorn and hotdogs	
Watching films on a big screen	
Sharing emotions with friends	
Enjoying the atmosphere	

(c) She says Danny Boon is her favourite French actor. What else does she say about him? State any **one** thing.

1

_____

(d) Why does she not like old French films? State any **two** things.

2

_____

_____

(e) Name any **two** advantages she gives of watching a film at home.

2

_____

_____

(f) What annoys her about French television? State any **two** things.

2

_____

_____

(g) Why does she like watching Channel 5? State **two** things.

2

_____

_____

[END OF QUESTION PAPER]

MARKS | DO NOT WRITE IN THIS MARGIN

ADDITIONAL SPACE FOR ANSWERS

MARKS | DO NOT WRITE IN THIS MARGIN

ADDITIONAL SPACE FOR ANSWERS

[BLANK PAGE]

DO NOT WRITE ON THIS PAGE

National
Qualifications
2015

X730/75/13

French
Listening Transcript

FRIDAY, 22 MAY

10:50 AM – 11:15 AM (approx)

This paper must not be seen by any candidate.

The material overleaf is provided for use in an emergency only (eg the recording or equipment proving faulty) or where permission has been given in advance by SQA for the material to be read to candidates with additional support needs. The material must be read exactly as printed.

Instructions to reader(s)

For each item, read the English **once**, then read the French **three times**, with an interval of 1 minute between the three readings. On completion of the third reading, pause for the length of time indicated in brackets after the item, to allow the candidates to write their answers.

Where special arrangements have been agreed in advance to allow the reading of the material, those sections marked **(f)** should be read by a female speaker and those marked **(m)** by a male; those sections marked **(t)** should be read by the teacher.

(t)   **Item Number One**

Whilst in France you listen to a young actor who is speaking on a local radio station.

You now have one minute to study the questions for Item Number One.

(f)   Bonjour à tous. Je suis là aujourd'hui pour vous parler du festival international des films ainsi que de mon nouveau film.

Le festival a commencé il y a sept ans et chaque année il devient de plus en plus populaire.

Il dure une semaine et il y a beaucoup de films à voir. Vous pouvez acheter un billet pour 30 euros qui vous donne le droit d'aller voir 20 films de votre choix.

Les avantages d'assister au festival sont nombreux. Les films sont en version originale et donc vous pouvez faire la connaissance de différentes cultures et améliorer votre compréhension des langues étrangères.

Après quelques films il y aura la possibilité de participer à un débat. Vous aurez l'occasion de donner votre avis sur le film, rencontrer les acteurs et aussi de vous faire de nouveaux amis.

Cette année vous pourrez voir le film dans lequel j'ai joué. Mon film raconte l'histoire d'une française qui commence une nouvelle carrière en Espagne. Il est à la fois drôle mais aussi émouvant. Je ne vous en dis pas plus, venez le voir. A bientôt.

(2 minutes)

(t) Item Number Two

Christophe talks to Julie about French cinema and television.

You now have one minute to study the questions for Item Number Two.

(m) Bonjour Julie, comment ça va?

(f) Ça va super bien. C'est le début des vacances et en plus c'est mon anniversaire alors tout va bien.

(m) Génial! tu as des projets pour ce soir ?

(f) Oui, je vais aller au cinéma avec mes copains.

(m) Tu aimes le cinéma ?

(f) Oui, j'adore ça. J'y vais au moins une fois par semaine. Il n'y a rien de mieux que de regarder des films sur un grand écran et de partager ses émotions avec des amis.

(m) Quels genres de film préfères-tu ?

(f) Je n'ai pas de genre préféré mais mon acteur français préféré est Danny Boon. Il me fait vraiment rire et j'aime son accent du nord de la France.

(m) Y-a-t-il des films que tu n'aimes pas ?

(f) Je n'aime pas tellement les vieux films français. Ils sont toujours trop longs, le langage utilisé est très démodé et il y a très peu d'action.

(m) Aimes-tu regarder les films à la maison aussi ?

(f) Je préfère aller au cinéma mais il y a des avantages à regarder les films à la maison aussi. Si on n'aime pas le film on peut changer de chaîne, si on veut aller aux toilettes on peut le pauser et bien sûr c'est gratuit.

(m) Aimes-tu regarder la télé ?

(f) Ça dépend. Ce qui m'énerve à la télé française, c'est qu'il y a des publicités toutes les dix minutes, qu'il y a trop de feuilletons américains et que tous les matins il y a énormément de jeux stupides.

(m) Y-a-t-il quand même quelques bonnes émissions à la télé?

(f) Oui, j'aime regarder la 5. On peut y voir des documentaires très intéressants et ce que j'aime le plus, c'est qu'il y a souvent des émissions en allemand.

(m) Oh c'est bien ça, je devrais la regarder moi aussi. Ecoute, je te souhaite de bonnes vacances et bien sûr un joyeux anniversaire.

(2 minutes)

(t) End of test.

Now look over your answers.

[END OF TRANSCRIPT]

Page three

[BLANK PAGE]

DO NOT WRITE ON THIS PAGE

NATIONAL 5
2016

N5

National
Qualifications
2016

Mark

X730/75/01

**French
Reading**

MONDAY, 16 MAY

1:00 PM — 2:30 PM

Fill in these boxes and read what is printed below.

Full name of centre

Town

Forename(s)

Surname

Number of seat

Date of birth

Day   Month   Year   Scottish candidate number

Total marks — 30

Attempt ALL questions.

Write your answers clearly, in **English**, in the spaces provided in this booklet.

You may use a French dictionary.

Additional space for answers is provided at the end of this booklet. If you use this space you must clearly identify the question number you are attempting.

Use **blue** or **black** ink.

There is a separate question and answer booklet for Writing. You must complete your answer for Writing in the question and answer booklet for Writing.

Before leaving the examination room you must give both booklets to the Invigilator; if you do not, you may lose all the marks for this paper.

MARKS | DO NOT WRITE IN THIS MARGIN

Total marks — 30

Attempt ALL questions

Text 1

You read the following article about Paris Plage, a beach in the centre of Paris.

Chaque été depuis treize ans, un coin de Paris se transforme en plage de sable fin sur la rive droite de la Seine*.

C'est vraiment un lieu pour tout le monde: par exemple, les enfants peuvent participer aux concours des châteaux de sable ou faire voler des cerfs-volants et les adultes peuvent tout simplement se détendre au soleil en lisant un livre.

Il y a un écran géant en face de la plage pour ceux qui ne veulent pas rater les événements sportifs de l'été.

Olivier, 18 ans, est grand fan de la plage de la capitale. Il dit, «C'est génial pour les jeunes parisiens parce qu'il y en a beaucoup qui n'ont pas la possibilité d'aller au bord de la mer. Ils peuvent aller à cette plage sans quitter Paris. L'année dernière, j'y suis allé chaque après-midi pendant les grandes vacances. C'était un bon point de rencontre pour moi et mes amis et c'était gratuit!»

Farid n'est pas d'accord. «Paris Plage n'est pas une vraie plage car on n'a même pas le droit de se baigner. Je préférerais aller à une station balnéaire ou à une piscine en plein air.»

la Seine* – the name of the river in Paris

Questions

(a) Complete the sentence. ①

There has been a beach in Paris every summer for

13 years .

(b) The beach has something for everyone.

(i) What is there for children? State **two** things. ②

· Sandcastle competition

· Fly kites

MARKS | DO NOT WRITE IN THIS MARGIN

Text 1 Questions (continued)

(b) (continued)

(ii) What can adults do there? State any **one** thing.   1

Read a book while they relax in the sun.

(c) There is also a giant screen. Who can benefit from this?   1

People who want to watch the summer sport events.

(d) Olivier thinks that the beach is great for young Parisians. Why?   2

Not many young Parisians have the possibility of going to the beach. They can go to this beach without leaving Paris.

(e) Olivier went to the beach every afternoon last year. What does he say about it? State any **one** thing.   1

It was a good meeting point for him and his friends

(f) Farid says Paris Plage is not a real beach.

(i) Why does he think this?   1

You're not allowed to swim

(ii) What would he prefer to do? State any **one** thing.   1

Go to an open air swimming pool

[Turn over

MARKS | DO NOT WRITE IN THIS MARGIN

Text 2

You read an article about life in the city and in the countryside.

De nos jours il y a beaucoup de gens qui cherchent à vivre à la campagne. Ils veulent passer plus de temps à l'extérieur et se sentir plus en sécurité.

Mais est-ce que cette vie est vraiment meilleure que la vie en ville?

Voici un témoignage de Cécile qui a vécu les deux vies.

«Je viens d'un petit village mais je n'aimais pas y vivre. Il n'y avait rien à faire pour les jeunes, donc je m'ennuyais beaucoup.

Donc à l'âge de 17 ans je suis partie pour trouver du travail en ville. J'ai toute de suite adoré la vie en ville. J'aimais le fait que personne ne me connaissait et qu'il y avait un choix de divertissements. Mais après quelques années, j'ai changé d'avis. La circulation commençait à m'énerver et j'étais toujours pressée.

J'ai donc décidé d'acheter une maison secondaire à la campagne et je ne le regrette pas. J'ai deux chiens qui adorent courir dans les champs et je peux oublier tous les soucis de la vie quotidienne.

Personnellement je crois que ma situation est idéale car je mène une vie équilibrée. Je profite de l'animation de la ville et de la tranquillité de la campagne.»

Questions

(a) Why do many people want to live in the countryside? State **two** things.   2

_____

_____

(b) What does Cécile say about the small village where she lived? Tick (✓) the correct statement.   1

Everyone knew everyone.	
She was really bored.	
There were not many young people.	

MARKS

Text 2 Questions (continued)

(c) Cécile moved to the city when she was 17. What did she like about city life at first? State **two** things.

2

_____

_____

(d) In what ways did her opinion of city life change after a few years? State any **one** thing.

1

_____

_____

(e) She has no regrets about having bought a house in the country. Why? State **two** things.

2

_____

_____

(f) Why does she think she has a good balance in her life now? State **two** things.

2

_____

_____

[Turn over

MARKS | DO NOT WRITE IN THIS MARGIN

Text 3

You read an article where a student, Michel, talks about work experience.

Je suis étudiant à la faculté de droit et comme la plupart des étudiants j'ai fait un stage en entreprise chaque été. C'est un moyen d'avoir de l'expérience pratique et de gagner un peu d'argent.

Cependant, trouver un bon stage n'est pas toujours facile. On a une chance sur deux de tomber sur un stage "perte-de-temps". Dans certaines entreprises on a trop de responsabilités tandis que dans d'autres on sert le café, c'est tout. En même temps, quand on est stagiaire*, il est parfois difficile de gérer de nouvelles tâches.

Moi, j'ai fait deux stages bien différents. Le premier était épuisant et en plus, le patron était toujours de mauvaise humeur et j'avais peur de poser des questions si j'avais un problème. Par contre, le deuxième stage était une expérience positive. J'ai appris énormément de choses, j'ai assisté aux réunions importantes et on m'a donné des conseils régulièrement.

Enfin, ayant parlé avec d'autres stagiaires et après mes propres expériences, je peux affirmer que la qualité du stage dépend du responsable de la formation.

*stagiaire = person doing work experience

Questions

(a) How does Michel describe work experience? Complete the following sentence. **2**

It is a way of _____

and _____ .

(b) Why it is not always easy to find a good work placement? State any **two** things. **2**

_____

_____

(c) What do those doing work experience sometimes find difficult? **1**

_____

_____

MARKS

DO NOT WRITE IN THIS MARGIN

Text 3 Questions (continued)

(d) Michel goes on to describe his two work placements.

(i) As well as being exhausting, what does Michel say about his first placement? State **two** things.

2

_____

_____

(ii) What made Michel's second placement a positive experience? State any **two** things.

2

_____

_____

(e) What is Michel's overall opinion of work experience? Tick (✓) the correct statement.

1

It is a waste of time and you are not paid any money.	
It is the only way of getting a job abroad.	
It can be a positive experience but it depends on the company.	

[END OF QUESTION PAPER]

MARKS | DO NOT WRITE IN THIS MARGIN

ADDITIONAL SPACE FOR ANSWERS

Page eight

MARKS | DO NOT WRITE IN THIS MARGIN

ADDITIONAL SPACE FOR ANSWERS

[BLANK PAGE]

DO NOT WRITE ON THIS PAGE

N5

National Qualifications 2016

Mark ☐

X730/75/02

French Writing

MONDAY, 16 MAY
1:00 PM — 2:30 PM

Fill in these boxes and read what is printed below.

Full name of centre

Town

Forename(s)

Surname

Number of seat

Date of birth

Day	Month	Year	Scottish candidate number

Total marks — 20

Write your answer clearly, in **French**, in the space provided in this booklet.

You may use a French dictionary.

Additional space for answers is provided at the end of this booklet.

Use **blue** or **black** ink.

There is a separate question and answer booklet for Reading. You must complete your answers for Reading in the question and answer booklet for Reading.

Before leaving the examination room you must give both booklets to the Invigilator; if you do not, you may lose all the marks for this paper.

MARKS | DO NOT WRITE IN THIS MARGIN

Total marks — 20

You are preparing an application for the job advertised below and you write an e-mail in **French** to the company.

Employeur: Chocolaterie 'Les délices charentaises'

Titre du Poste: Vendeur/vendeuse

Profil: Accueillir et conseiller les clients, aider à la caisse, ranger la boutique, savoir parler l'anglais et le français.

Renseignements: Pour plus de détails, contactez

Mme Laurent au courriel: chocolaterie.delicescharentaises@gmail.com

Adresse: 38 rue du Château
18570 Graves Saint -Amant

Tél: 05 43 92 06 34
Fax: 05 43 92 06 35

To help you to write your e-mail, you have been given the following checklist.

You must include **all** of these points

- Personal details (name, age, where you live)
- School/college/education experience until now
- Skills/interests you have which make you right for the job
- Related work experience
- The dates you would be available to work there
- Ask a question about the job.

Use all of the above to help you write the e-mail in **French**. The e-mail should be approximately 120–150 words. You may use a French dictionary.

MARKS DO NOT WRITE IN THIS MARGIN

ANSWER SPACE

Bonjour! Je m'appelle Hannah et j'ai quinze ans.
Je suis née à Edinbourg et j'y habité pendant
deux ans. Maintenant, c'est à Fortrose que j'habite.
Ma ville se trouve dans le nord-est d'Écosse près
du Loch Ness. Ce que j'aime dans mon village c'est
qu'il y a beaucoup de choses dont une
bibliothèque et un centre de loisirs.

Je suis élève de Fortrose Academy, et je suis en
seconde. J'ai choisi six matières dont le français,
l'allemand et l'anglais. Ma matière préféré c'est
l'allemand parce que la ~~proff~~ ~~proffe~~ ~~professeure~~
professeure est vraiment sympa et gentille et car
j'aime la langue. J'étudie aussi le gaélique
mais pas dans l'~~éo~~ école.

Je me decrirais comme étant une personne
honnête et travailleuse. Je m'entends très
bien avec ~~beaucou~~ beaucoup de gens et j'
adore parler aux autres. J'ai aussi
beaucoup de patience et résilience.

Je n'ai jamais travaillé mais je suis bénévole
pour Fortrose Guides. J'aide les filles de 9

ANSWER SPACE (continued)

à 14 ans avec activités. Ces activités sont chaque semaine dans la mairie. Un jeu traditionnel c'est le "spoon Game" - c'est ~~tou~~ toujours drôle!

Je peux travailler apres ~~la~~ mes examens et quand je ne suis pas en école. Je suis libre pour la ~~plou~~ plupart des vacances d'été car je ne vais nulpart. J'ai hâte de travailler avec vous!

Mon question c'est: ~~comment~~ combien autre gens vais travaillais avec moi?

MARKS | DO NOT WRITE IN THIS MARGIN

ANSWER SPACE (continued)

MARKS | DO NOT WRITE IN THIS MARGIN

ANSWER SPACE (continued)

[END OF QUESTION PAPER]

MARKS | DO NOT WRITE IN THIS MARGIN

ADDITIONAL SPACE FOR ANSWERS

MARKS | DO NOT WRITE IN THIS MARGIN

ADDITIONAL SPACE FOR ANSWERS

FOR OFFICIAL USE

N5

National
Qualifications
2016

Mark 16/20
80%

X730/75/03

**French
Listening**

MONDAY, 16 MAY

2:50 PM — 3:20 PM (approx)

Fill in these boxes and read what is printed below.

Full name of centre

Town

Forename(s)

Surname

Number of seat

Date of birth

Day	Month	Year	Scottish candidate number

Total marks — 20

Attempt ALL questions.

You will hear two items in French. **Before you hear each item, you will have one minute to study the questions.** You will hear each item three times, with an interval of one minute between playings. You will then have time to answer the questions before hearing the next item.

You may NOT use a French dictionary.

Write your answers clearly, in **English**, in the spaces provided in this booklet. Additional space for answers is provided at the end of this booklet. If you use this space you must clearly identify the question number you are attempting.

Use **blue** or **black** ink.

You are not allowed to leave the examination room until the end of the test.

Before leaving the examination room you must give this booklet to the Invigilator; if you do not, you may lose all the marks for this paper.

MARKS | DO NOT WRITE IN THIS MARGIN

Total marks — 20

Attempt ALL questions

Item 1

Jean, a French student, speaks about a school exchange.

(a) When does Jean's school come to Scotland? State any **one** thing.   ①

One week in spring.

(b) Which personal details do pupils have to give their teachers before signing up for the exchange? State any **two** things.   ②

Any pets and diet/eating habits.

(c) The pupils go to the Scottish school every morning. What other activities do they do:

(i) in the afternoon? State any **two** things.   ✗ 1

Attraction park / tour of village

(ii) in the evening with their host family? State any **one** thing.   ①

Eat scottish specialities

(d) What did Jean particularly love about Scotland? State any **one** thing.   ✗

The people were very chivalrous. (welcoming?).

(e) What is the **main** benefit of taking part in a school exchange? Tick (✓) the correct statement.   ①

It is a good way to get to know another country well	✓
You spend time away from home	
You have the opportunity to go away with your friends	

MARKS | DO NOT WRITE IN THIS MARGIN

Item 2

Jacques talks to Monique about her recent school exchange experience in Scotland.

(a) Why is Monique tired? State **two** things.   2

_After the flight of hours she was on in
car ride
a ~~plane~~ that lasted 24 hours and it's very busy in
scotland._

(b) Monique talks about the differences in the Scottish school.

(i) What does she say about the school facilities? State any **one** thing.   ①

• _Big sports ~~fixed fost~~ field_

(ii) Why does she think Scottish pupils are lucky? State any **two** things.   ②

• _They have less homework_
• _They can do activities after school_

(c) Monique took part in lessons in Scotland.

(i) What happened in the history class? State any **one** thing.   ✗

• _They made an animation._

(ii) Why did she really enjoy the Spanish class? State **two** things.   ②

• _The teacher was passionate about the subject_
• _He explains lessons well_

(d) What did she not like about the school? State any **two** things.   ②

• _There wasn't much choice in the cateen_
• _They only have time to eat a sandwich._

[Turn over

MARKS | DO NOT WRITE IN THIS MARGIN

Item 2 (continued)

(e) What does Monique say about school uniform? Tick (✓) the two correct statements.

2

It is smart	✓
It is not expensive	
The pupils feel proud when they wear it	✓
It is not popular with the pupils	

[END OF QUESTION PAPER]

MARKS | DO NOT WRITE IN THIS MARGIN

ADDITIONAL SPACE FOR ANSWERS

MARKS | DO NOT WRITE IN THIS MARGIN

ADDITIONAL SPACE FOR ANSWERS

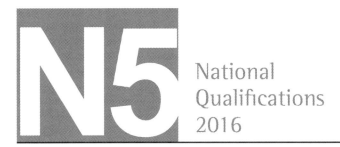

National
Qualifications
2016

X730/75/13

French
Listening Transcript

MONDAY, 16 MAY
2:50 PM — 3:20 PM (approx)

This paper must not be seen by any candidate.

The material overleaf is provided for use in an emergency only (eg the recording or equipment proving faulty) or where permission has been given in advance by SQA for the material to be read to candidates with additional support needs. The material must be read exactly as printed.

Instructions to reader(s)

For each item, read the English **once**, then read the French **three times**, with an interval of 1 minute between the three readings. On completion of the third reading, pause for the length of time indicated in brackets after the item, to allow the candidates to write their answers.

Where special arrangements have been agreed in advance to allow the reading of the material, those sections marked **(f)** should be read by a female speaker and those marked **(m)** by a male; those sections marked **(t)** should be read by the teacher.

(t)   Item Number One

Jean, a French student, speaks about a school exchange.

You now have one minute to study the questions for Item Number One.

(m)   Bonjour, je m'appelle Jean. Je vais vous parler de l'échange scolaire dans mon école. Tous les ans, nous passons une semaine au printemps en Ecosse.

Avant le séjour, chaque élève donne quelques détails personnels aux professeurs. Par exemple, des informations sur ses passe-temps, ses animaux domestiques, et s'il y a des choses qu'on n'aime pas manger. Ensuite, les profs essaient de mettre ensemble les élèves écossais et les élèves français qui partagent les mêmes intérêts.

A l'étranger, on loge chez son correspondant. Les journées sont très chargées. On passe les matinées en cours au collège. L'après-midi on va au parc d'attractions, on achète des cadeaux pour des amis ou on fait un tour de la ville. Le soir on reste en famille où on a l'occasion de goûter des spécialités du pays et on discute des événements de la journée.

J'ai vraiment adoré mon séjour en Ecosse. Les gens étaient vraiment chaleureux et le paysage était impressionnant. J'espère y retourner très bientôt. Je recommanderais un échange à tout le monde.

(2 minutes)

(t)   **Item Number Two**

Jacques talks to Monique about her recent school exchange experience in Scotland.

You now have one minute to study the questions for Item Number Two.

(m)   Salut Monique, tu es bien rentrée de ton échange scolaire?

(f)   Ça va merci mais je suis toujours un peu fatiguée après le voyage de vingt-quatre heures en car. En plus, on était vraiment occupé en Ecosse tous les jours.

(m)   Est-ce que tu as remarqué des différences au collège écossais?

(f)   Ben, oui. Il y avait beaucoup de différences. Par exemple, le bâtiment était bien équipé avec un grand terrain de sport. De plus les élèves écossais ont de la chance! Ils finissent les cours avant 16 heures, ils ont moins de devoirs et ils peuvent participer aux activités après l'école.

(m)   Est-ce que tu as participé aux cours?

(f)   Oui tous les jours. Par exemple en histoire il y avait un débat animé et on a fait des sondages. La leçon que j'ai aimée le plus était l'espagnol car le prof était passionné par sa matière et expliquait bien ses cours.

(m)   Est ce qu'il y avait des choses que tu n'aimais pas?

(f)   Ce que j'ai trouvé moins bien était que la pause-déjeuner était trop courte; la plupart des élèves avait juste le temps de prendre un sandwich. De plus il n'y avait pas beaucoup de choix à la cantine et les repas n'étaient pas équilibrés.

(m)   Et que penses-tu de l'uniforme scolaire?

(f)   Tiens, ça fait un look très habillé. C'est une bonne idée de s'habiller différemment pour travailler au collège. A mon avis, les élèves sont fiers de porter leur uniforme et de faire partie d'une communauté.

(m)   Ça a l'air très intéressant; je vais peut-être y aller l'année prochaine.

(2 minutes)

(t)   **End of test.**

Now look over your answers.

[END OF TRANSCRIPT]

[BLANK PAGE]

DO NOT WRITE ON THIS PAGE

NATIONAL 5

2017

FOR OFFICIAL USE

N5

National Qualifications 2017

Mark

X730/75/01

French Reading

MONDAY, 15 MAY

1:00 PM — 2:30 PM

Fill in these boxes and read what is printed below.

Full name of centre

Town

Forename(s)

Surname

Number of seat

Date of birth

Day	Month	Year	Scottish candidate number

Total marks — 30

Attempt ALL questions.

Write your answers clearly, in **English**, in the spaces provided in this booklet.

You may use a French dictionary.

Additional space for answers is provided at the end of this booklet. If you use this space you must clearly identify the question number you are attempting.

Use **blue** or **black** ink.

There is a separate question and answer booklet for Writing. You must complete your answer for Writing in the question and answer booklet for Writing.

Before leaving the examination room you must give both booklets to the Invigilator; if you do not, you may lose all the marks for this paper.

MARKS | DO NOT WRITE IN THIS MARGIN

Total marks — 30

Attempt ALL questions

Text 1

Whilst in France, you read an article for school pupils about group work.

Le travail en groupe

Savoir travailler en équipe est essentiel dans la vie professionnelle ainsi que la vie de tous les jours. Il est donc indispensable d'acquérir les compétences pour pouvoir travailler en groupe à l'école et voici quelques conseils pour bien s'organiser.

Comment former un bon groupe.

Il est important de choisir des camarades de classe avec une variété de compétences et de trouver des personnes motivées qui veulent travailler. Mais attention: se mettre en groupe avec ses meilleurs amis n'est pas toujours une bonne idée. On risque de ne rien faire car on passe le temps à bavarder ou à rigoler.

Comment éviter le conflit.

Les disputes sont parfois inévitables. Pour bien s'entendre il faut rester respectueux envers les autres, écouter les opinions de tout le monde et apprendre à faire des compromis.

Comment travailler d'une manière efficace.

Tout d'abord il faut diviser les tâches équitablement et chaque membre du groupe doit avoir un rôle spécifique. Pour avoir de bons résultats tout le monde doit faire de son mieux et rester positif.

Questions

(a) Team work is important. Complete the sentence.   1

Knowing how to work in a team is essential in your job as well as in

_____ .

MARKS | DO NOT WRITE IN THIS MARGIN

Text 1 Questions (continued)

(b) The article gives advice on forming a good group.

    (i) What is it important to do? State any **two** things.   **2**

_____

_____

    (ii) Why is it not always a good idea to go into a group with friends? State any **two** things.   **2**

_____

_____

(c) Arguments are sometimes inevitable. What can you do to avoid these? State any **two** things.   **2**

_____

_____

(d) The article goes on to discuss how to work effectively together. Give any **three** examples.   **3**

_____

_____

_____

[Turn over

MARKS | DO NOT WRITE IN THIS MARGIN

Text 2

Later, you read an article about heatwaves.

En France il est normal d'avoir du beau temps en été mais on parle de *canicule lorsqu'il fait extrêmement chaud. On peut dire qu'il y a une canicule quand les températures montent vite et la chaleur ne faiblit pas pendant soixante-douze heures.

Malheureusement les canicules arrivent de plus en plus. En 2003 la canicule a causé la mort de beaucoup de gens en France. Ce drame a fait scandale car le gouvernement a été accusé de ne pas avoir informé les Français des risques liés à la canicule.

Il est nécessaire d'aider les personnes qui souffrent de la chaleur, en particulier les personnes âgées et les jeunes enfants. Pour ne pas souffrir pendant la canicule il est recommandé de boire au moins deux litres d'eau par jour, de se mouiller les cheveux régulièrement et de ne pas faire trop d'exercice physique.

Pendant la période de canicule il vaut mieux rester à l'intérieur aux heures les plus chaudes. Si vous devez sortir, mettez un chapeau pour vous protéger la tête, essayez de rester à l'ombre ou allez aux endroits climatisés. A la maison gardez les fenêtres fermées pendant la journée pour que la chaleur ne rentre pas.

*canicule – heatwave

Questions

(a) The article describes what a heatwave is. Complete the sentence.   2

You can say there is a heatwave when temperatures increase

_____ and the heat doesn't go down for

_____ hours.

(b) What happened as a result of the heatwave in 2003?   1

_____

_____

MARKS | DO NOT WRITE IN THIS MARGIN

Text 2 Questions (continued)

(c) The French government received a lot of criticism. Why?   **1**

_____

_____

(d) The article recommends what you should do to avoid suffering during a heatwave. State **three** things.   **3**

_____

_____

_____

(e) The article gives further advice on how to cope during a heatwave.

   (i) What should you do if you have to go out? State any **two** things.   **2**

_____

_____

   (ii) What should you do at home? State **one** thing.   **1**

_____

_____

[Turn over

MARKS | DO NOT WRITE IN THIS MARGIN

Text 3

You also read an article about an interesting website.

Le stage en entreprise

Il est bien connu qu'un stage en entreprise apporte des avantages. Par exemple on apprend à gérer son temps et à travailler en équipe. Cependant il est souvent difficile de trouver un stage convenable.

Pour aider les étudiants en France le gouvernement a lancé le site www.monstageenligne.fr. Cela permet aux étudiants de trouver plus facilement un stage qui pourrait être utile pour leur future carrière. Ce site est avantageux pour les employeurs aussi parce qu'ils peuvent offrir les stages aux étudiants qui s'intéressent vraiment à leurs entreprises.

Alors le site est un succès? Voici l'expérience de David.

Quand j'avais 16 ans je voulais bien devenir cuisinier. Malheureusement mes parents ne pouvaient pas m'aider à trouver un stage car ils ne connaissaient personne dans ce domaine. Mais au lycée, mon prof de français m'a parlé du site et j'ai pu trouver un stage dans un restaurant renommé.

Après ce stage au restaurant, j'ai décidé que cette carrière n'était pas pour moi. Je trouvais les heures trop longues et on est debout toute la journée. Par contre il y avait des aspects positifs. J'ai pu développer mes compétences dans le monde du travail, j'ai plus de confiance en moi et je me suis bien entendu avec mes collègues.

Questions

(a) What are the advantages of doing work experience? Complete the sentence.

    1

You learn to _____ and to

work in a team.

MARKS | DO NOT WRITE IN THIS MARGIN

Text 3 Questions (continued)

(b) The French government has launched a website. How does it help:

   (i)   students? State any **one** thing.   1

   _____

   _____

   (ii) employers? State **one** thing.   1

   _____

   _____

(c) David talks about his experience of using the site. What job did he want to do when he was 16?   1

   _____

   _____

(d) Why were his parents not able to help him?   1

   _____

   _____

(e) David talks about his work experience.

   (i)   What decision did he come to after this work experience?   1

   _____

   _____

   (ii) What did he not like about the job? State **two** things.   2

   _____

   _____

   (iii) What were the positive aspects? State any **two** things.   2

   _____

   _____

[END OF QUESTION PAPER]

MARKS

DO NOT WRITE IN THIS MARGIN

ADDITIONAL SPACE FOR ANSWERS

MARKS DO NOT WRITE IN THIS MARGIN

ADDITIONAL SPACE FOR ANSWERS

[BLANK PAGE]

DO NOT WRITE ON THIS PAGE

N5

National Qualifications 2017

Mark

X730/75/02

French Writing

MONDAY, 15 MAY

1:00 PM — 2:30 PM

Fill in these boxes and read what is printed below.

Full name of centre

Town

Forename(s)

Surname

Number of seat

Date of birth

Day   Month   Year   Scottish candidate number

Total marks — 20

Write your answer clearly, in **French**, in the space provided in this booklet.

You may use a French dictionary.

Additional space for answers is provided at the end of this booklet.

Use **blue** or **black** ink.

There is a separate question and answer booklet for Reading. You must complete your answers for Reading in the question and answer booklet for Reading.

Before leaving the examination room you must give both booklets to the Invigilator; if you do not, you may lose all the marks for this paper.

MARKS DO NOT WRITE IN THIS MARGIN

Total marks — 20

You are preparing an application for the job advertised below and you write an e-mail in **French** to the company.

Hôtel Debrienne
Toulouse centre

Cherche (h/f) RECEPTIONNISTE

Profil: Anglais et français courant, bonne présentation, expérience dans l'hôtellerie souhaitée

Veuillez contacter: brienne@hoteldebrienne.com

To help you to write your e-mail, you have been given the following checklist. You must include **all** of these points:

- Personal details (name, age, where you live)
- School/college/education experience until now
- Skills/interests you have which make you right for the job
- Related work experience
- Information about your hobbies
- Ask any two questions about the job.

Use all of the above to help you write the e-mail in **French**. The e-mail should be approximately 120—150 words. You may use a French dictionary.

ANSWER SPACE

[Turn over

ANSWER SPACE (continued)

ANSWER SPACE (continued)

MARKS DO NOT WRITE IN THIS MARGIN

ANSWER SPACE (continued)

[END OF QUESTION PAPER]

MARKS | DO NOT WRITE IN THIS MARGIN

ADDITIONAL SPACE FOR ANSWERS

ADDITIONAL SPACE FOR ANSWERS

Page eight

FOR OFFICIAL USE

N5

National
Qualifications
2017

Mark

X730/75/03

**French
Listening**

MONDAY, 15 MAY

2:50 PM — 3:20 PM (approx)

Fill in these boxes and read what is printed below.

Full name of centre

Town

Forename(s)

Surname

Number of seat

Date of birth

Day	Month	Year	Scottish candidate number

Total marks — 20

Attempt ALL questions.

You will hear two items in French. **Before you hear each item, you will have one minute to study the questions.** You will hear each item three times, with an interval of one minute between playings. You will then have time to answer the questions before hearing the next item.

You may NOT use a French dictionary.

Write your answers clearly, in **English**, in the spaces provided in this booklet. Additional space for answers is provided at the end of this booklet. If you use this space you must clearly identify the question number you are attempting.

Use **blue** or **black** ink.

You are not allowed to leave the examination room until the end of the test.

Before leaving the examination room you must give this booklet to the Invigilator; if you do not, you may lose all the marks for this paper.

MARKS | DO NOT WRITE IN THIS MARGIN

Total marks — 20

Attempt ALL questions

Item 1

Audrey talks about her experience of sharing a flat.

(a) Audrey lives in a flat in Marseille.

    (i) Why does she like her flat? State any **one** thing.

        1

_____

_____

    (ii) What are the disadvantages? State any **one** thing.

        1

_____

_____

(b) Audrey decided she wanted to share her flat. What type of person did she want to live with? State any **two** things.

    2

_____

_____

(c) Sophie became Audrey's flatmate.

    (i) After a few months they started to argue. What did they argue about? State any **two** things.

        2

_____

_____

    (ii) They decided to talk to each other about their problems. Why are things better now? State any **two** things.

        2

_____

_____

MARKS | DO NOT WRITE IN THIS MARGIN

Item 2

Nathalie speaks to Benoît about his weekend at his grandparents'.

(a) Where do Benoît's grandparents live? State any **one** thing.   **1**

_____

_____

(b) What does he say about their house? Tick (✓) the **two** correct statements.   **2**

	Tick (✓)
It has a very big garden	
It is an old house	
There are 3 bedrooms	
There is a motorway nearby	

(c) What is the village like? State any **two** things.   **2**

_____

_____

(d) He says he wasn't bored at his grandparents' house. What did he do with them:

   (i) on Saturday? State any **two** things.   **2**

     _____

     _____

   (ii) on Sunday? State any **two** things.   **2**

     _____

     _____

[Turn over

MARKS | DO NOT WRITE IN THIS MARGIN

Item 2 (continued)

(e) Benoît gets on well with his grandparents. How does he describe them? State any **two** things.

2

_____

_____

(f) Why did he have an argument with his grandfather when he was 18? State **one** thing.

1

_____

_____

[END OF QUESTION PAPER]

MARKS | DO NOT WRITE IN THIS MARGIN

ADDITIONAL SPACE FOR ANSWERS

Page five

MARKS | DO NOT WRITE IN THIS MARGIN

ADDITIONAL SPACE FOR ANSWERS

National
Qualifications
2017

X730/75/13

French
Listening Transcript

MONDAY, 15 MAY

2:50 PM — 3:20 PM (approx)

This paper must not be seen by any candidate.

The material overleaf is provided for use in an emergency only (eg the recording or equipment proving faulty) or where permission has been given in advance by SQA for the material to be read to candidates with additional support needs. The material must be read exactly as printed.

Instructions to reader(s):

For each item, read the English **once**, then read the French **three times**, with an interval of 1 minute between the three readings. On completion of the third reading, pause for the length of time indicated in brackets after the item, to allow the candidates to write their answers.

Where special arrangements have been agreed in advance to allow the reading of the material, those sections marked **(f)** should be read by a female speaker and those marked **(m)** by a male; those sections marked **(t)** should be read by the teacher.

(t) Item Number One

Audrey talks about her experience of sharing a flat.

You now have one minute to study the questions for Item Number One.

(f) J'habite un appartement à Marseille dans le sud de la France. J'aime bien mon appartement car il se trouve à 5 minutes de mon travail et il y a beaucoup de magasins à proximité. Le seul inconvénient est que mon appartement se trouve au 4ème étage et il n'y a pas d'ascenseur.

Il y a un an j'ai décidé de partager mon appartement car je n'aimais pas vivre seule. Je voulais vivre avec quelqu'un de mon âge, qui ne fume pas et qui a les mêmes intérêts que moi. J'ai donc passé une annonce dans le journal et après quelques entretiens j'ai trouvé Sophie.

Au début tout s'est très bien passé entre Sophie et moi. Mais après quelques mois on a commencé à se disputer de plus en plus. Sophie ne faisait pas de tâches ménagères, elle faisait trop de bruit et elle laissait toujours les lumières allumées.

Heureusement qu'on a décidé de se parler et de résoudre nos problèmes. Maintenant Sophie fait la vaisselle, elle invite ses amis seulement le week-end et elle essaie d'économiser l'électricité. On est à nouveau de très bonnes amies.

(2 minutes)

(t) **Item Number Two**

Nathalie speaks to Benoît about his weekend at his grandparents'.

You now have one minute to study the questions for Item Number Two.

(f) Bonjour Benoît, comment ça va?

(m) Salut Nathalie, je vais très bien merci. Je viens de passer un week-end chez mes grands-parents.

(f) Ils habitent où?

(m) Ils habitent un petit village près de Lyon.

(f) Elle est comment la maison?

(m) Super chouette. C'est une vieille maison avec une belle piscine. Ce que je n'aime pas c'est qu'il y a une autoroute juste à côté et on entend la circulation qui passe. Mais on s'y habitue.

(f) Et c'est comment le village?

(m) Bien, bien. C'est tranquille mais il y a un bon réseau de transport en commun et des bus réguliers pour aller en ville.

(f) Et tu ne t'es pas trop ennuyé?

(m) Pas du tout. Il faisait super beau. Samedi, on a passé la journée à se baigner dans la piscine et à bronzer et puis le soir on a fait un barbecue sur la terrasse. C'était vraiment sympa. Dimanche matin, mon grand-père et moi sommes allés à la pêche. A midi on a mangé au restaurant et plus tard on a fait une petite promenade aux alentours.

(f) Alors tu t'entends très bien avec tes grands-parents?

(m) Ah oui je m'entends très bien avec eux. Ils sont très jeunes d'esprit, très actifs pour leur âge et je peux leur parler de tout. J'ai de la chance de les avoir.

(f) C'est bien ça. Et vous ne vous êtes jamais disputés?

(m) Oui une fois quand j'avais 18 ans. Je venais de passer mon permis de conduire et j'ai pris la voiture de mon grand-père sans demander la permission. Mon grand-père était vraiment en colère mais je me suis excusé et maintenant on en rigole.

(f) Il a l'air cool ton grand-père. J'aimerais bien le rencontrer un jour.

(m) La prochaine fois que je vais chez eux, viens avec moi, si tu veux.

(f) Merci ça serait sympa.

(2 minutes)

(t) **End of test.**

Now look over your answers.

[END OF TRANSCRIPT]

[BLANK PAGE]

DO NOT WRITE ON THIS PAGE

NATIONAL 5

Answers

NATIONAL 5 FRENCH 2015

Reading

Text 1

(a)
- (Her) clothes (any spelling)/garments
- a trip/a holiday/journey/travelling
  (NB – Clothes and holiday interchangeable)

(b)
- Asked her **mum's friend/a friend of her mum** (who has a shop)
- Called/phoned/asked/spoke to the (boss) of a (big) company

(c) To wait/come back/return in two/three years. (Both numbers do not need to be mentioned)/Come back in a couple of years/when she is 17/18.

(d) *Any two from:*
- During the school holidays
- (Only if) the school holiday lasts two weeks/15 days/14 days (or more).
- **Cannot/can't/not allowed to** work **more than** five hours **a day/daily/in the daytime OR can only** work five hours **a day/daily/in the daytime** etc.

(e)
- Do/help with housework/cleaning/household chores/chores for an **old(er)/elderly** person
- Give (individual/particular/private) lessons/courses/tutoring to (younger) pupil(s)/student(s)/children/ help younger people with school work/tutor/teach younger people
- **Mow/cut** the lawn/garden/grass

Text 2

(a) The Internet is an essential tool at work (Second box ticked)
(NB – More than one box ticked = 0 marks)

(b) *Any two from:*
- Do/helps with research/investigations
- communicate with people/students **from around/ all over/across the world/abroad/everywhere/ anywhere**
- learn computer skills/learn computing

(c) *Any one from:*
- The child/the student/the pupil can find help/ information/do it (himself/on his own/instead of asking parents) **OR** they/he/she can find information/help **themselves/himself/on their own**
- The parent/they can get/give/find information for/ **to inform the child**

(d) (i) *Any one from:*
- You can lose (any recognisable spelling) contact/touch with reality/real world
- You read less/fewer books

(ii) (Stay at home) to chat/discuss/talk/speak with virtual friends/virtually/on the computer/ internet/online.

(iii) Do not **believe** everything (you read/see/ someone says/writes) (on the internet) **OR** Not everything (you read) (on the internet) is **true/ correct.**

(e) *Any two from:*
- There are not **enough computer(s)** (in each classroom/room/class).
- The computer/system/network/data system/IT (often) does not work/breaks down
- Difficult/hard to **access/reach/get on to/find** (interesting/web/some) sites/some sites are not **accessible.**

(f) The Internet can support learning when and where appropriate
(Third box ticked)
(NB – More than one box ticked = 0 marks)

Text 3

(a) **Perfect** apples

(b) (i) (They have to make/pick/choose) a strict selection (process)/select strictly/strictly select

(ii) Fruit (and) vegetables/produce with (the slightest) **things wrong/problems/defects/flaws/ with a bit of damage/which are off/not perfect/ which aren't up to standard/scratch/good enough** go in the bin/get thrown away/wasted.

(c)
- Buy more than they eat/need/consume/buy too much food/produce/products
- (In France) **20%** of food is thrown away/wasted/put in the bin
  (NB – We buy more than we eat by 20% = 2 marks)

(d) *Any two from:*
- Money used in/on food/fruit and veg **production** is wasted/Money we use **to produce** food/fruit and veg is wasted
- Waste/scrap has to be treated/dealt with/processed/ necessary to treat/process waste/recycled
- Recycling uses/requires/needs/demands (a lot of) energy

(e)
- (Make/have/use/write) a shopping list/a list of shopping
- (Only) buy/get/purchase the right quantity/ amount/produce/food/stuff needed/necessary/ required. **OR** Don't buy unnecessary/too many products/more than you need.
- (You can) freeze **leftovers/scraps/food that's left/ the rest/what you don't eat** (in the fridge)

Writing

Candidates will write a piece of extended writing in the modern language by addressing six bullet points. These bullet points will follow on from a job-related scenario. The bullet points will cover the four contexts of society, learning, employability and culture, to allow candidates to use and adapt learned material. The first four bullet points will be the same each year and the last two will change to suit the scenario. Candidates need to address these "unpredictable bullet points" in detail to access the full range of marks.

Category	Mark	Content	Accuracy	Language resource — variety, range, structures
Very good	20	The job advert has been addressed in a full and balanced way. The candidate uses detailed language. The candidate addresses the advert completely and competently, including **information in response to both unpredictable bullet points.** A range of verbs/ verb forms, tenses and constructions is used. Overall this comes over as a competent, well-thought-out and serious application for the job.	The candidate handles all aspects of grammar and spelling accurately, although the language may contain one or two minor errors. Where the candidate attempts to use language more appropriate to Higher, a slightly higher number of inaccuracies need not detract from the overall very good impression.	The candidate is comfortable with the first person of the verb and generally uses a different verb in each sentence. Some modal verbs and infinitives may be used. There is good use of adjectives, adverbs and prepositional phrases and, where appropriate, word order. There may be a range of tenses. The candidate uses co-ordinating conjunctions and/or subordinate clauses where appropriate. The language of the e-mail flows well.
Good	16	The job advert has been addressed competently. There is less evidence of detailed language. The candidate uses a reasonable range of verbs/verb forms. Overall, the candidate has produced a genuine, reasonably accurate attempt at applying for the specific job, **even though he/she may not address one of the unpredictable bullet points.**	The candidate handles a range of verbs fairly accurately. There are some errors in spelling, adjective endings and, where relevant, case endings. Use of accents is less secure, where appropriate. Where the candidate is attempting to use more complex vocabulary and structures, these may be less successful, although basic structures are used accurately. There may be one or two examples of inaccurate dictionary use, especially in the unpredictable bullet points.	There may be repetition of verbs. There may be examples of listing, in particular when referring to school/ college experience, without further amplification. There may be one or two examples of a co-ordinating conjunction, but most sentences are simple sentences. The candidate keeps to more basic vocabulary, particularly in response to either or both unpredictable bullet points.

Category	Mark	Content	Accuracy	Language resource — variety, range, structures
Satisfactory	12	The job advert has been addressed fairly competently. The candidate makes limited use of detailed language. The language is fairly repetitive and uses a limited range of verbs and fixed phrases, e.g. *I like, I go, I play*. The candidate copes fairly well with areas of personal details, education, skills, interests and work experience but does not deal fully with the two unpredictable bullet points **and indeed may not address either or both of the unpredictable bullet points.** On balance, however, the candidate has produced a satisfactory job application in the specific language.	The verbs are generally correct but may be repetitive. There are quite a few errors in other parts of speech — gender of nouns, cases, singular/plural confusion, for instance. Prepositions may be missing, e.g. *I go the town*. Overall, there is more correct than incorrect.	The candidate copes with the first and third person of a few verbs, where appropriate. A limited range of verbs is used. Sentences are basic and mainly brief. There is minimal use of adjectives, probably mainly after is e.g. *Chemistry is interesting*. The candidate has a weak knowledge of plurals. There may be several spelling errors, e.g. reversal of vowel combinations.
Unsatisfactory	8	The job advert has been addressed in an uneven manner and/or with insufficient use of detailed language. The language is repetitive, e.g. *I like, I go, I play* may feature several times. There may be little difference between Satisfactory and Unsatisfactory. **Either or both of the unpredictable bullet points may not have been addressed.** There may be one sentence which is not intelligible to a sympathetic native speaker.	Ability to form tenses is inconsistent. There are errors in many other parts of speech — gender of nouns, cases, singular/plural confusion, for instance. Several errors are serious, perhaps showing mother tongue interference. The detail in the unpredictable bullet points may be very weak. Overall, there is more incorrect than correct.	The candidate copes mainly only with the personal language required in bullet points 1 and 2. The verbs "is" and "study" may also be used correctly. Sentences are basic. An English word may appear in the writing. There may be an example of serious dictionary misuse.

Category	Mark	Content	Accuracy	Language resource — variety, range, structures
Poor	4	The candidate has had considerable difficulty in addressing the job advert. There is little evidence of the use of detailed language. Three or four sentences may not be understood by a sympathetic native speaker. **Either or both of the unpredictable bullet points may not have been addressed.**	Many of the verbs are incorrect. There are many errors in other parts of speech — personal pronouns, gender of nouns, cases, singular/plural confusion, prepositions, for instance. The language is probably inaccurate throughout the writing.	The candidate cannot cope with more than one or two basic verbs. The candidate displays almost no knowledge of the present tense of verbs. Verbs used more than once may be written differently on each occasion. Sentences are very short. The candidate has a very limited vocabulary. Several English words may appear in the writing. There are examples of serious dictionary misuse.
Very poor	0	The candidate is unable to address the job advert. **The two unpredictable bullet points may not have been addressed.** Very little is intelligible to a sympathetic native speaker.	Virtually nothing is correct.	The candidate may only cope with the verbs to have and to be. Very few words are written correctly in the modern language. English words are used. There may be several examples of mother tongue interference. There may be several examples of serious dictionary misuse.

Listening

Item 1

(a) 7 years ago/2008

(b) *Any one from:*
- To see/watch **20** films/up to **20** films
- To see film(s) of your choice/to see film(s) you like/ prefer

(c) *Any one from:*
- (Get to know/appreciate/see/learn about/explore/ understand/experience) different culture(s)/ (it shows/introduces) different culture(s)/ other countries' culture(s)/new culture(s)/(see) differences in other culture(s)
- Improve your (understanding of) (foreign) language(s)/understand language(s)/learn different/ new language(s)/familiarise yourself with other language(s)/great for learning language(s)

(d) *Any two from:*
- Give your opinion about/view on the film/talk about how good the film was
- Meet/interview/question/speak/talk to (the) actor(s)
- Make/meet (new) friend(s)

(e) *Any one from:*
- A (French) woman/man/person/someone who starts a (new) career/job (in Spain)/finding a (new) career/job (in Spain)
- A (French) woman/man/person/someone who goes to/moves to/is **in Spain**/lives **in Spain**

(f) To promote international films
(Second box ticked)
(NB – More than one box ticked = 0 marks)

Item 2

(a) *Any one from:*
- It is the (beginning of)/she is on/going on holiday(s)/vacation
- It is her birthday

(b) • Watching films on big screen
- Sharing emotions
(Second and third boxes ticked)
(NB – 3 boxes ticked maximum 1 mark; 4 boxes ticked = 0 marks)

(c) *Any one from:*
- He makes her laugh/he's (really/truly) funny
- She likes his accent (from the North of France)/She enjoys his accent/She likes the way he speaks/He has a nice/good accent
- He has an accent from the North (of France)/is from the North (of France)/was born in the North (of France)/lives in the North (of France)

(d) *Any two from:*
- They are **too/very/quite/really** long
- The **language** used is old-fashioned/out of date/not modern/ancient
- Not a lot of/little/no **action**/not much happens/not good **action**/(very) slow/boring

(e) *Any two from:*
- Change the channel/ programme/movie/film/it/ watch something else (if you don't like it)
- **Pause/Stop** it to go to the **toilet/bathroom**
- It is free/no charge/you don't have to pay

(f) *Any two from:*
- (Lots of/too much) **advertising**/(too many/lots of) **advert(s)/commercial(s)** (every 10 minutes/are long) **adverts** every 2 minutes
- (Too many) **American** soap(s)/series/sitcom(s)/ show(s)/programme(s)/it's all **American**/it's like **American** TV/**American** TV show(s) are stupid
- (A lot of) stupid game show(s)/quiz(zes) **OR** game show(s)/quiz(zes) **in the morning OR stupid programme(s)/thing(s) in the morning/every morning**

(g) • **Interesting documentaries/documentary** (any recognisable spelling)
- Programmes in **German/from Germany/German** programmes

NATIONAL 5 FRENCH 2016

Reading

Text 1

(a) Thirteen/13 **year**(s)

(b) (i) • Sand castle (building)**competition**(s)/**contest**(s)
    • (Fly) kite(s)/kite flying

   (ii) *Any one from:*
       • *Relaxing* **in the sun**
       • Reading/read (a book)

(c) Those/people who don't want to miss the **sporting events**/people who (want to/enjoy/rather) watch/see **sporting events** (in the summer)
People who enjoy sporting events

(d) • (Lots/many of them) don't have the **chance/ possibility/opportunity** to go/**can't** go to the sea(side)/beach
    or
    Gives them/they have the **possibility** to/ **opportunity/chance to** go/they **can** go to the beach
    • (They can go) **without leaving/don't need to leave** Paris

(e) *Any one from:*
    • *(Great/good) meeting place/point/spot for him and his* **friends**/he can hang out with his **friends**
    • It is/was free/he (and his friends)/me (and my friends) can go there for free/they don't have to pay/it doesn't cost.

(f) (i) **Not allowed to/not possible to/do not have the right to/can't** swim/bathe/go bathing there

   (ii) *Any one from:*
       • Go to a **sea**(side) resort/the **sea**(side)
       • Go to an **outdoor** pool/pool **in the fresh/open air**

Text 2

(a) • Spend/pass (more) time **outdoors/outside**
    Like to be outdoors
    • To feel/it is safe(r)/(more) secure/has a sense of security

(b) She was bored
(Second box ticked)

(c) • That no one knew her/people didn't know her/she knew no one/didn't know anyone
    • A **choice/selection** of entertainment/**a lot of/plenty of/various** things to do

(d) *Any one from:*
    • The traffic began/started to **annoy/irritate her/get on her nerves**/the traffic **is annoying/irritated her/ annoyed her**
    • **She** was (always) rushed/in a rush/hurry (everyday)

(e) • (Two) dogs (love) **running** in the field(s)/the countryside
    • **Forget** the worries/concerns/problems of **every day/daily** life/she doesn't have to worry about **everyday** life/leaves her **daily** worries behind

(f) • (Take advantage of/benefit from) the bustling **city/ town life**/the busyness/the liveliness of the **city/ town**
    • Quiet/peaceful (life) **in the country(side)**/ tranquillity of **the country(side)**

Text 3

(a) • Having/getting **practical/hands on/useful/helpful/ right** experience
    • Earning/gaining/making/(a little/a bit of) money

(b) *Any two from:*
    • (One in two chance of a placement) being a waste of time/it can be a waste of time
    • (In some/certain companies you have/there are) **too many/much/lots of** responsibilities
    • (In other/some companies you (only/just) serve/ make coffee

(c) Managing/doing/handling **new** tasks/du**ties**

(d) (i) • **The boss/manager** was (always) in a bad mood
       • He was **scared/frightened/afraid/found it difficult/struggled** to ask questions (if he had a problem)

   (ii) *Any two from:*
       • He learned lots/an enormous/tremendous amount (of things)/he was taught a lot
       • He attended/went to (important) meetings
       • He was given/they gave him advice (regularly)

(e) It can be a positive experience but it depends on the company
(Third box ticked)

Writing

Please see the assessment criteria for Writing on pages 100–102.

Listening

Item 1

(a) *Any one from:*
    • (In) spring
    • Every year/(one week) every year/once a year

(b) *Any two from:*
    • Their hobbies/interests/pastimes/things you like/ are interested in
    • Their animals/pets/animals in their house/ household animals/domestic animals
    • If there are things/foods/is anything they **don't** like eating/to eat/**can't** eat

(c) (i) *Any two from:*
       • Go to a theme park/amusement park/fairground
       • Buy/shop for/get **presents/gifts/souvenirs** (for friend(s))
       • Visit/tour of the town/city, walk around the town/city/town tour(s)

   (ii) *Any one from:*
       Chance to
       • Taste/try specialities **of the country/region/ area/Scotland**, eat a traditional/special **Scottish** meal, **national** speciality foods
       • Talk/discuss/speak/tell/chat about/share (the events of) the/his/her/their **day**/how the **day** went/what happened during the **day**

(d) *Any one from:*
- The people/locals/Scottish (people)/Scots
- Scenery/countryside/landscape/the views

(e) It is a good way to get know a country well
(First box ticked)

Item 2

(a) • **24 hour** (coach/bus) journey/ride/she was travelling for **24 hours**
or
Long coach/bus journey/ride
- She was (really) busy/(really) occupied/it was busy (in Scotland) (every day)/she did a lot (of activities) (when she was there)

(b) (i) *Any one from:*
- (The building/school/it was) well-equipped
- **Big/large sports** ground(s)/pitch(es)/(playing) field(s)/area(s)/space(s)

   (ii) *Any two from:*
- Finish/school ends/finishes before/at/by 4pm/16.00
- **Less** homework/**not as much** homework
- (Can take part/participate in) activities/clubs/ **at the end of the day/after school**/extra-curricular activities

(c) (i) *Any one from:*
- (Lively/animated) debate/argument/discussion
- Did survey(s)/questionnaire(s)

   (ii) • Teacher was passionate/enthusiastic/excited (about subject) really likes/loves (the subject)
- Explained/explains well/explained/explains the lesson(s)/everything/it (well)/teacher was good at explaining

(d) *Any two from:*
- The lunch/dinner break is (too/very) short/not long (enough)/not as long/shorter
- **Just/only** (enough) **time** to eat a sandwich
- Not enough/not a lot of/not much/no choice in the canteen/there aren't many options in the canteen
- Meals/menu/food/canteen not balanced/unbalanced/not healthy

(e) • It's smart
- They feel proud
(First and third boxes ticked)

Reading

Text 1

(a) Everyday/daily/day to day life/life everyday.

(b) (i) • (Choose/pick/have) (classmate(s)/friend(s)/ people/pupil(s) with) different/a variety/mix of skill(s)/competence(s)/capabilitie(s)/knowledge
- Find motivated people/person
OR
- People who are motivated to work/want to work/like working/work well.

   (ii) *Any two from:*
- Do nothing/not doing anything/not on task/ don't get the work done/not working
- Chat/talk/speak/gossip
- Laugh (a lot/too much)/having a laugh/joke/ fun.

(c) *Any two from:*
- (Be) respectful/respect others
- Listen to (everyone's) opinion(s)/others
- (Learn how to/make) compromise.

(d) *Any three from:*
- Divide the task(s) equally/evenly
- Everyone has a specific/different role/task/job/ specify roles
- Do your best/one's/their best
- Stay/remain/be positive.

Text 2

(a) • Quickly/quick/fast
- 72/seventy two.

(b) Many/a lot of/numerous people died/death(s).

(c) Did not inform/tell/warn/give advice to (the French/ France) of/about the risk(s)/danger(s).

(d) *Any three from:*
- Drink (at least/more than) two litres of water a/per day/don't drink less than 2 litres of water a/per day
- Soak/wet/moisten your hair (regularly)
- Don't do/avoid too much/many/a lot of (physical) exercise/sport
- Stay in at the hottest time/hour(s).

(e) (i) *Any two from:*
- Wear/put on a hat/cap
OR
- Protect/cover your head
- Stay/rest in the shade/shadow(s)
- Go to air conditioned place(s).

   (ii) Close/shut your windows/keep your windows closed/shut during the day/for the day/all the day.

Text 3

(a) Manage (one's/your) time.

(b) (i) *Any one from:*
- To find a (work) placement/work experience/ training (course) (more) easily/easier
- Useful/helps/helps prepare for their future career.

(ii) • They can offer work <u>placements/training (course)/experience</u> to students
OR
• They can find students who are interested/have an interest in their <u>business/company/firm/ enterprise</u>.

(c) Cook/chef.

(d) • Didn't know <u>anyone/someone</u> in this/that/the <u>field/ job/line of work/area of work/domain</u>
OR
• Didn't know any/a chef/cook.

(e) (i) Job/it/this/being a chef/this career wasn't for him/he didn't want to be a chef.

(ii) • Long hours
• On your feet/standing (up)/stood (up) <u>all day/ the whole time/the whole day/all the day</u>.

(iii) *Any two from:*
• Developed/gained <u>skills/competences/ capabilities/abilities/knowledge</u> (in the world of work)
• Became/has become confident/increased in/ gained in/improved/developed/gave him confidence
OR
• He is <u>more</u> confident/he has <u>more</u> confidence
• Got/gets on well with colleagues/likes working with his colleagues.

Writing

Please see the assessment criteria for Writing on pages 100–102

Listening

Item 1

(a) (i) *Any one from:*
• <u>5 minutes</u> from (her) <u>work/her job</u>
• A lot of/lots of/many shops
OR
• Shops <u>near(by)/close/near</u> the shops.

(ii) *Any one from:*
• On 4th floor/4th storey (accept any spelling)
• No lift/elevator/she has to walk up (stairs).

(b) *Any two from:*
• Same/similar age
• Doesn't smoke/non-smoker/shouldn't smoke
• Same/similar interests/likes same/similar things/ same things in common.

(c) (i) *Any two from:*
• The housework/housekeeping/chores/cleaning/ tidying/helping around the house/flat
• The noise she/Sophie made (a lot of/too much) noise/she was noisy/she was (too) loud/there was (a lot of/too much) noise
• The light(s) left on/light(s) not turned off/ light(s) always on.

(ii) *Any two from:*
• <u>Sophie/she</u> does the washing-up/dishes
• (She/they) (only) invite(s) friends/people at the weekend/friends come at the weekend
• (She/they) <u>save(s)/conserve(s)/economise(s)/ use(s) less/do(es) not waste/do(es) not use as much</u> electricity/energy.

Item 2

(a) *Any one from:*
• <u>A small/little</u> village
• <u>Near</u> Lyon (accept any spelling).

(b) • It is an old house (box 2)
• There is a motorway nearby (box 4).

(c) *Any two from:*
• It is quiet/peaceful/calm/tranquil (accept any spelling)
• There is (a lot of/loads of) (good) (public) transport
• Bus/coach goes/buses/coaches go to <u>town/city (centre)</u>
OR
• <u>Regular</u> bus(es)/coach(es)/bus(es)/coach(es) come(s) <u>regularly</u>/there are <u>many/a lot of</u> buses/ coaches.

(d) (i) *Any two from:*
• Swimming/going to/in (swimming) pool
• Sunbathing/tanning/tan
• (Had) a barbecue/BBQ (on terrace).

(ii) *Any two from:*
• Fishing/fish
• (Went to a) restaurant
OR
• Went out to eat/out for lunch/out for dinner
• (Went for a) (small) <u>walk/walked</u>.

(e) *Any two from:*
• Young at heart/young spirited/youthful/act young
• (Very) active (for their age)
• He/You can talk/speak to them (about anything)
They are good to talk/speak to/easy to talk to
They can talk (to each other) about anything
• (He is) lucky to have them.

(f) <u>Took/drove</u>/used grandfather's/his/their car (without permission/asking).

Acknowledgements

Permission has been sought from all relevant copyright holders and Hodder Gibson is grateful for the use of the following:

Image © CREATISTA/Shutterstock.com (2015 Reading page 2);
Image © Pressmaster/Shutterstock.com (2015 Reading page 4);
Image © SasPartout/Shutterstock.com (2015 Reading page 6);
Image © ever/Shutterstock.com (2016 Reading page 2);
Image © vvoe/Shutterstock.com (2016 Reading page 4);
Image © David Hughes/Shutterstock.com (2016 Reading page 4);
Image © Ioannis Pantzi/Shutterstock.com (2016 Reading page 6);
Image © LuckyBusiness/stock.adobe.com (2017 Reading page 2);
Image © prajwal/stock.adobe.com (2017 Reading page 4);
Image © wavebreakmedia/stock.adobe.com (2017 Reading page 6).